A Wayfarer's Poems:
The Mirror

A Wayfarer's Poems: The Mirror

T. A. GIBSON

RESOURCE *Publications* · Eugene, Oregon

A WAYFARER'S POEMS: THE MIRROR

Resource Publications
An Imprint of Wipf and Stock Publishers
199 W. 8th Ave., Suite 3
Eugene, OR 97401

www.wipfandstock.com

PAPERBACK ISBN: 979-8-3852-2561-3
HARDCOVER ISBN: 979-8-3852-2562-0
EBOOK ISBN: 979-8-3852-2563-7

VERSION NUMBER 09/12/24

Creativity does best proclaim
that no one else has done it this way.

CONTENTS

The Mirror

A DAY ON EARTH

begins anew
as sight of it
appears to humans:

hilly, billowing
in a blue-silver sea,
hues of heather

imbue the turning earth
as afternoon brings
warmth to time passing,

and reticence is best
as evening climbs
east to west

out of reach
of sentient beings
and their needs,

grasping for life
as ticking kings
on a sphere in time

where nothing
beautiful
will escape alive—

if only we
could live in peace
as days abate

and pass from an earth
inhabited with conflict,
then night arrives.

A RELIQUARY

In a reliquary all that we are,
or ever were, persists remembering
the reveries and moments lived
that add up to make us:

yesterdays of impassivity,
temperance and tenderness,
victories of prominence
and learning how to greet them;

ecstasies of adolescent noesis
and its ignorance of contentment,
loving but for the feeling,
wild with willful self-conceits;

learning just to comprehend
there is so much we do not know,
and reckoning with fate that all we are
our parents did not make.

In similes and dreams there are friends,
relatives, who we will never see again
and each decade faces change,
but ours to us look the same—

then in the end we realize
in just a box so much does fit,
and such is life when it is full,
we are not here to open it.

ABSENCE OF LOVE

With a little light
ten minutes of touching
comes and goes,

others with their intent
and you with yours—
it gets mixed

into the event,
and the part of life
where two become one.

Amities and likes
align instead
with family and friends,

and while time is a passing tick,
our problems are indigenous
and fraught with self-interests.

Other than this,
through life we covet
many splendid things,

and trek the days
and the years away,
confident in their continuance,

never thinking of
what the absence of love does
that always conspires to end them.

ALL AMERICA

("America does not repel the past or what it has produced under its form or amid other politics or the idea of castes or the old religions . . . accepts the lesson with calmness . . . is not so impatient as has been supposed that the slough still sticks to opinions and manners and literature while the life which served its requirements has passed into the new life of the new forms . . . perceives that the corpse is slowly borne from the eating and sleeping rooms of the house . . . perceives that it waits a little while in the door . . . that it was fittest for its days . . . that its action has descended to the stalwart and well-shaped heir who approaches . . . and that he shall be fittest for his days."

Leaves of Grass, *Preface to the 1855 Edition,* *Walt Whitman)*

"All America, Walt, is not well.
The song of myself is of words,
and but a dirge to the end
of what it represents, and
should I craft it truly
and consider it a treatise,
its truth must first be apprehended
by a need, or an alignment with
the many ways people believe."

"All America, Walt, great and good
is not what it was when war tore at its soul
over liberty in the union, or
in states' independence—still liberty
must have its limits to keep the peace,

and now, ten times more people mid
our shores exist but cannot agree
on what is right, how to live,
or even on what is important!"

"All America, Walt, is not aligned,
our existence is being redefined:
all, in some way, are uniquely different
but should be treated the same
and given equal opportunity
to become who they are and live freely,
and legislation cannot change
how we are made,
only how we should be perceived."

"All America, Walt, perhaps will fall
because of its greatest principals awarded to all,
and like all other nations that promoted freedom,
will be torn apart by the extents of its people,
and left to be grieved in the annals of history—
but as for me I cannot agree
with far left or right ideologies,
and dare to maintain that there are better ways
to honor this land—the great and grand America!"

ALTERNATIVE MEANS

It's an alternative we have,
technology:

to think we tweet,
to feel we watch movies;

to talk we text,
to touch we use emoji;

to meet we create profiles
to match compatibility;

to socialize we chat in real-time,
to remember we take pictures;

to read we listen
to what is said from talking things;

to write we type,
to agree we click *Like*.

All love their lives,
palpably, or online—

the difference is now we
are enriched scientifically,

and can live out our lives
through alternative means.

ANGELIC ONES

There are manners
of human conditions
where ignorance abounds
as we exhibit them;

ways birthed of evil
that never parts
as long as what we want
is deified above God.

It seems that we
live in-between
the good that we are
and the bad that we need.

There are desires
that we cannot shun,
so much a part of who we are
that they dash—they run:

    a look
    I want
    your lips
    kiss good;

    to give
    purely
    as such
    in love;

a little
girl
to smile
like yours.

Through the course of life,
love is embossed
so wondrously
upon our souls

that we know not of
where it is from,
and scarce what for
until we succumb.

What is more,
through His unmerited favor,
we are granted presence
with the Lord forever—

where the night is not,
and our needs are undone,
we shall become
angelic ones.

ANOTHER POET GROWING OLD

(To Ezra Pound)

"Ezra, I sit tonight eating chicken
cut up into grammatical pieces
with my fork held oppositely
in my left hand so I can write:

each word is a nibble,
each sentence is a bite.

My thought surrounds each gulp
with its incessant saliva
welling up in my mouth
in an empty booth around me,

I sit spelling rabid
inside Patsy's dinner lounge.

People are glaring at me writing,
lips moving, molars grinding,
chewing concepts—
Ezra, they think,

they think I'm weird,
as I produce paragraphs!

Should I tell them of your ideogrammatic
method, and its heaping up of all
vorticism into coherent meaning?
Should I ask them,

"Hast'ou seen the rose
in the steel dust of thought?"

I will tell them! And then insistent tell myself
that your being judged mentally incompetent
was only because of the illiterate ignorant,
and in the end brilliance, I have yet to show,

immured in a sanatorium,
another poet growing old."

AWAKENING

Meandering
   from simple to serene,
   the brush of dawn is
ushering

   nightly tales
   of recollections

fresh
   from dreaming to day needs
   making these moments
motionless

   in brevity,
   and yet infinite

remembering
   that simplicity's adversary
   evades peace as life
glistens

   through a plain glass
   windowpane that your

looking
   out through the cracks in time
   and slices of age peering to
perceive.

BECOMING

Graceful peace
pours inwardly,
purging past
our last miss,

madly made
differently than
the way we seek
the truth now openly.

Clear are inflections,
night balances day, and
God never takes the verity
He blessed us with away;

then when we are calm,
our flesh having fallen
humbled in submission
shedding at the altar,

we confess what
should not persist,
but then the life we live
is spent repeating this—

and to have truly
died to self
is only when
we have left earth.

BELONGING

Those terms in time
when we were the same
were grouped into years,

before changing again
as moments slipped
into memories, and

conversations were simpler,
uttered in nativity,
before we became

what we believed,
and lived our lives
accordingly.

If we knew,
forgive the thought,
as much as You,

we would but hasten
our demise into eternity—
so now we lay hours away

sessiled to time,
and with but our faith
we belong.

DENIZEN'S DAYS

Eons amply made,
none the same,
have passed on their intent:

lives lived,
histories spent,
urban, rural, mixed;

hunters gathering,
centuries,
accounts of victories

jotted into annals,
Herodotus, Tacitus,
Greco-Roman-ness.

Humans each made
the essence of their ages
unique in implement

as kingdoms and dynasties
came and went—
while the essence of life,

the immediate
doesn't ever senesce,
then it is gone

and epochs subsist
amid mortals
woven as stitches—

denizens' days
will only go away
with the tale of time.

ELD TOO EARLY

Eld is time's last behest:
the passing through never the same,
slow in youth, quick with age;

'tis suddenly we there arrive
from times of innocence
through ontology's decline;

strange we were made eonian,
then perfectly placed, corporeal,
inside a live aging capsule.

Only in the flesh does eld exist,
an interval of evermore
that we spend on earth content;

though this I praise in a written fit,
I must object—
"I'm it too early!"

GONE AWAY

To have gone away
and sent yourself there:

in nether-lands
obsession brings
what you want
but not the way you want it,

and when stumbling
from drinks, the floor awaits
as a welcoming fate,
but not as a good time.

Others have gone away
crumpled in malintent:

an accident severing
life from limbs
takes hence tenderness,
and lying in a still interim

through memories
you're life you live,
while hope is now
only God's to give.

To have gone away,
would you know it:

in a mind's minute
an inherent tendency
could lend life distance
in a space of wilderness

indigent of the harmony
of night and day—
but what would near be
without far away?

GOOD OF ME

My time is flying past earthliness:
essential loveliness,
friends then, I miss.

The way I love is different today,
though with whom
close by remains.

Only the good of me do others see,
but I am aberrant,
rarely serene.

I can never get there, or far enough
away from man—
Im one of them.

Some things I have become, I cannot run
from their affinities,
or the straight-edge

schizophrenia that's balancing them
as unwell urgings
with the good of me—

I try to change, but they are family
and are quite content
to waste time spent—

yet there is a fight to the death of them,
for they are alarmed
at not being passed on.

It seems I can live with these maladies—
but I cannot die
with them being me!

IN UNITY

It starts while young,
the love of life,
becoming you
while befriending others.

Predilections you find
while never knowing from
which relative you got them,
or why you look like just one.

Soon enough you are the result
of the things you've done,
and affect others as you discover
the remiss of selfishness.

In life there are consequences
for everything we do,
and if we respect differences
we can live as we were intended to.

INTO THE EXTENT

Enclosed in a concrete airport
many races convene,
following signs and smart-screens
to a gate to get a seat
on a polished cylindrical
identifiable flying thing;

now at 34,000 feet
minus 50 degrees feels fabulous,
and someone in a uniform
is smiling, disbursing
a savory trail mix
of freeze-dried fragments,
salted, with food coloring—

suddenly the Linux kernel
in front of me is flashing,
and a digital display with a brain
indicates were 6,000 miles away;

shuddering, shaking,
through strata of space,
water or something
has been displaced
into the atmosphere, and
particles of it disappear
into white fume—

so close to death
in our seats we exist,
lulled, ticketed,
absconding into the extent.

JUST WAIT TO BE PERFECT

Slices of life peal from time
in a continuum in a cauldron,
and every ten years a batch of them
are kept and memorialized,
having ended then, we just remember if
they were okay, or something went wrong;

faces fade, and flashing back
to better times in the course of our cause,
each dawn fills the air with light,
dreams devise, and we move on.

Decades become the way they were
while we consider how to get better,
amass more money, and look lovelier
as we socially ascend
and compete as spectacles
of the what we can achieve—

suddenly, we arrive withering
with all of our accolades of self-interest,
and realize that we have missed the little things
and life has past—just wait to be perfect!

LAST BIRTHDAY

I believe in better, beautiful things
that men scarce seek, that are not me;

    existing on earth temporarily
    the grieving edge is strange,
    when pushed past it
    every time brings change,

and when the umbra of darkness has left,
its leaving breaks hell-bad woes

    slicing life from death
    as steel severs stone
    the end of these things
    is a beginning it seems,

where sharing laughter with friends
brings joy as you are renewed,

    like children
    Christmas morning
    brings to
    make them smile—

God's gifts are what we open now
until thousands more arranged await,

    and heaven's hands
    with stars arrayed
    begin their work
    on our last birthday.

LIBERTIES

are never just given, and
if you were born into them,
others before have lost their lives
to keep you free;

humanity has never lived in harmony,
six thousand years ago, today,
different ways to the same end,
with hoards to slaughter

and kill indiscriminately,
it's always a mix
of good and evil
and those who suffer from it

just to live freely
amidst oppression—so sad
it is that human dignity
is not distributed equally,

and what does it mean
to live in peace
when there are always others
ready to take away your liberties?

LIFE

like the sea on earth is temporary,
and rolls with waves of countless lives

    under the sky
    not knowing why,
    it covers us all
    as half of a whole;

our human-produced wars are old,
and yet we live with what we oppose

    until by the end
    we have become
    what we have loved,
    and our fate begins

when marveling we can't pretend
there is no God trembling before Him

    at eternities' behest
    will be forested Elysium,
    or an abyss to drop off
    to a second death.

LIFE LANDING

Fiction is to believe
that in your wants
you see your needs
through myths, fables,
dreams, or fantasies;

the in-betweens
of the nether regions
then become living entities.

Reality occurs,
or was factually perceived
as time ushers existence
in periodic allotments
that cannot be changed,

and what has ended
then becomes mundane
as a part of the past.

Shakespeare to Morrison,
Lord Byron to Huxley—
there are no limits
to the psyche's abilities,
only to sanity, and

we are here but for an interim,
two sides of a soul,
tossed twirling, life landing.

LITTLE ME

I began there before I was my own,
and evenings never set me free;

no evening ever passed without form,
or moist movement, or mystic pleas,
and there in an ignorant innocence
I passed like wine through good intent.

I saw the ways that I was not,
and understood in little bits
when I was small in smaller towns,
now I am grown, in cities now.

I watched the night from day devour
thin light slowly into darkness.

I was not before, and I never was not
in the mind of God where lives are tilled
in providence—how do I know,
how could I doubt, that we are wisps

of what we'll be—now I am flesh,
soon I am dust, time will purvey
the future similarly for all on earth
where I grow old, a little me.

LOST LIFE

(for David)

A year-stick we took
to measure lost life:
the first, the last,
then the summed average;

not through conscious cause,
but with a heart-hollowed
need to pay respects,
to move on, words were spoken

and thoughts poured
from indexed slides
of pictures and songs loved
by a friend, now gone.

The shadows of death
in the bright lights dimmed,
and the sky fell down
to encompass them

as we passed through memories,
looking back we were remiss,
and time is so veiled
when it no longer exists.

LOVE IS

Love one:
    ordained before,
    perfectly planned,
    with different depths
    misunderstood;
    special bond of
    spirit and flesh,
    togetherness
    superseding
    the arcs of time
    and forever
    in a manner
    God wills and weaves.

Love two:
    youth becoming
    the attraction;
    blue, beautiful,
    blond and loving;
    first time and first
    love that I would
    die for after
    losing it, I
    hadn't a doubt
    I could never
    live without it
    and the passion.

Now all
    likeness since then,
    projected as
    love was really
    one, though at first

it was two, and
I persist in
being drawn to
others who look
like them in some
way, and as the
years pass I live
remembering.

To wait
    is a cruel fate,
    and a likely
    thing to do if
    both are lost and
    love is true, it's
    not only just
    about them now—
    could no other
    expect any
    of this, or love
    someone whose heart's
    left divided.

MAXIME MANEO

(L. The Greatest that Remains)

Pleasure is *a priori,*
or more to the point
what we want,

for with an orb
to ogle is not
beauty adored,

and to think
that love is thought
is heterodox.

Perception is *a posteriori,*
or mental like a want
turned inside out

upon its cause,
that is if you thought,
otherwise what you saw

or your senses brought,
a feeling felt,
is what it was.

Beliefs are absolute
truths to humanity
that develop quite naturally,

maxime maneo,
and whether infallible
or instilled wrong

are arbiters of all
holy writs or human blather,
and in the end, all that matter!

MEANTIME

our desires we crave—
to keep them bottled,
put the corkscrew away.

Time only permits, it does not govern
or elicitlike love that made us do that,
and we are now what has happened in the past.

Time is no advocate of human lives,
and it does not stop to father
us with insight concerning what we've done
wrong,

or to let the mirror render
the future without the hauntings,
the faintest longings for things we've thrown
away—

it's always passing,
it's only passing,
it's always only passing.

METRO-FALL

Boundaries of asphalt,
highwayed city limits,
metros enclose masses
incarcerated within them:

the names of the streets
intersect with red and green,
and people can't walk
without signs directing them

      as the sound of rain
      peals off pavement,
      high-rise buildings
      and nature-less things;

nights lit with fulgor fume
and bellow from metal
machines that pollute the air
for those living on the streets

to breathe, and overpasses
serve as roofs for the destitute
to look up at from the concrete
floors they sleep on

      as increased population
      breeds inverse probity,
      and things not locked
      become public property,

and to provide for the populace
using less space, the sky
is scraped with steel mitts
to award avarice with appearances—

people, despite all of this,
preferably or palsied persist
as the progeny of large cities
in a metro-fall of humanity.

MIX

Never mix
lust with blue;
red is not
love's passion to spill

the better's essence,
and biting bits
of pretty pulp
is selfish.

Never mix
what it is
that brown eyes
don't bruise

if they cannot
be kept for yours
with indifference
that does not esteem.

Never mix
what you hold true today
with vagaries
of time's intent

to make you ancient
and remove them
if you did not desire
their death ever dearly.

Never mix
what you do not have
with an excuse to offend,
or think someone else

fulfills this reverie when
you can live without it
you are better prepared
for eternity.

MULTIPLICITY

We love the world,

> the blond lies,
> sometimes
> it is the truth

> adultery belies
> if we said
> we cared,

and it was what we felt

> as time slipped
> past secrets kept,
> we were just maddened,

> deprecated, fresh-dead
> from repeated replication
> of the same things—

but still we suffer

> from lack of relief,
> desires lived out
> as desperate needs,

> and multiplicity's
> the balm the Enemy
> uses to woo

us with pretty things

    that others own
    that we feel for
    until they're gone—

    and hell can be had
    through many of these
    on earth before we leave!

MYTHLAND

I have arrived as a new being.
I feel, see, and breathe the air
that surrounds me—I can perceive
but do not understand, there is something

    warm, light, colors, and
    I touch things curiously
    and like or disapprove
    of everything around me

    while making it known
    as I turn toward noises
    and effects that alter
    my immediate needs;

    I have no knowledge
    of who I am, but
    there is a sense
    that I belong

    to who keeps holding
    me, and removing
    pieces of clothing
    that fit snuggly.

I manifest and grow physically,
emotions rule my life—I cry,
I scream, and view the world
according to what I want and need.

My actions have consequences
it seems, that some are good and
some are bad, and some affect the lives
of others who constantly surround me.

As I grow sensations come,
others just go, and feelings now
not just for me begin to surface
as anomalies, yet they are normal things.

I look persistently, eccentricities
are perceived as comeliness,
and manifest as affectionate
pleas to consummate in them.

I am being drawn to another
who is not like me, who
does different things, looks better
and is pleasant to see,

and when we are together
I am more than just me
as feelings come as a flood
that I must swim in or drown

and become another someone
who took and never gave,
and now resides in a grave
having given a tombstone their name.

I now have fantasies
that manifest in moods,
and play out as fiction
of my present situations

in interludes music with words
aptly describe, so vividly,
needs of mine that ravage time
and are changing me:

songs outwardly
affect me
subconsciously
and define my life;

excitement is
a beat away,
and catalysts
I use for this

just make me fly
and then forget
I left the ground
only to come down

as day drenches
what I'm seeking
with a new morn
to keep searching.

Memories, most of them,
are unimportant
but just keep happening
as I live in the moments spent.

II

You start to think logically,
reasoning after you've perceived,
to ascertain what just occurred
to determine why and what for;

your mind is alive
assimilating things,
and there is little time
to organize them into meaning;

you live in time-bound vicissitudes,
and are for now, truly free,
as you have little responsibilities
in the world you are just now discovering:

you can't stop soaring
from lack of things
to learn,

and instinct always
serves you better
apart

than emotion does,
as you'll never
suffer

forever from a
flash of insight
like love.

So many things have become evident,
what you felt was the first of them,
but now a recognition of prominence,
a realization occurs

that you are better than others
in many ways, an individual
to be coveted as a unique
specimen of a human being

who does not need what can be exceeded
by personal means without the necessity
of others who are not a part
of your eminence, now clearly obvious,

but arrogance comes with a price,
and as you wonder whether,
but know no better, you begin
to lose things in your life,

and what does not agree
with your ideology holds no truth
objectively when you cannot
love opposite self-deceit—

but you
cannot keep
what you
do not honor,

and truly have
become lost
when you're dreams
are as messed up

as you are,
and a vow
that is broken
mars time,

for there is
only once
for the love
of your life,

and only when you've realized
your brevity can you pretend
to acknowledge that your life on earth
will end, and all that will be left of you

are children, and after them
faded photographs, or digital bits
in files in directories on devices
with thousands of others with similar endings.

III

Some concerned have done great things,
and amassed great wealth and belongings
for themselves and their posterities,

but many more just simply exist
without expectations or entanglements
to make it through each day alive, and

ironically it is much more difficult
to have everything, for we lose part of it
each day on our way to perpetuity,

and too often we consent
to permit dying men their wishes,
and they go to hell the way they want.

There is a loveliness that pertains to eternity,
a certainty of knowing that we will meet God,
if only briefly, to greet His majesty,

and it will not matter who we were,
a president or a pauper,
but rather, how we treated others.

We do not know what we will become,
but from the mind of God, to conception,
through our lives on earth, then eternity—

we are,

and live in the moments until they expire
for there will be eons enough in forever,
and those of us not raptured alive

will die,

but not all of us will have truly lived—
yet those of us who are full of regrets
absolutely know that we have done so,

for the whole of life is not all good,
and earthly existence is transient—
as we are joined here together

only briefly,

until our shells have become the dust
of our days, and our spirits as singletons,
unique and infinite, are swept away

to gaze upon the wonderous One
who made all living beings,
the universe, and the heavenlies—

"Lord, if you will it,
let the lives of all
be reconciled

for the good concerned,
and not be a disgrace
left in a grave;

oversee us not
to be reckoned
with execration

O Keeper of
pure peace and
deific ways—"

for we are just wayfarers, never there,
only seeking our dreams, changing,
as hints of immortality define our lives

fresh rain falls, and recurring tendencies resume
in a mythland, as new as revelation seems,
we've all been cast—limitless, sentient beings!

NEVER-WAS

Posterity insists that
you cannot dismiss it
if misfit in the course of cause
all your worth is yours alone;

if you cannot smile
when a mirror's gone,
descending from
but never to anyone.

Pliny the Younger
no one remembers
except that he was a lawyer,
and died writing letters—

posterity-less
you die like this:
all that you are
just future intent

that will never become
anything but a lifetime of
peering veneration
for the never-was!

NO MAN

No man have I ever known:
philia, eros, or was ever close
or a kindred friend to me;

good times before,
and acts adored
would make it seem so to most,

but if made He men
to avoid being alone
then where is he,

my yokefellow,
or father, or mentor
of a common call?

It's only in time
where the divisions of men
doth dishonor our cause:

the marrow, the essence
of our Father's toil
is inside, while

the liquor'd pout
of a loud mouth
will never confess

what can't be stopped
isn't blessed,
waiting for when

we don't need
what we continue to do
during the rest of the week—

no wonder no man
have I ever known,
scantly even part of my own soul!

NO TIME

Too many days have crossed the sky
and fled into time, their nights have
beguiled me so dearly in dreams;

decades have become numbered things,
different entities, ever changing with
central themes that weave tapestries.

Old company is rarely a welcoming,
and in abject absence memories
fade into the oblivion of what was:

    who am I now
    that I was not,
    having changed from
    what you forgot,

    and who are you
    to have become
    so different
    from who you were?

It's easy to not care about others
that you do not know, and there are so
many friends that have disappeared,

and now moribund it is much
easier to just persist with what's left,
not what's gone, as there is no time anymore—

but today broke bright in the home
that I have ended up in, and I woke
remembering the friends that I have known.

NEO-THINGS

I've seen a spear so silvery
could scarce discern the sky from it,
but sail it will from point to tail,
its passengers content to marvel not

at theory bared, or glee to glide—
"just get us there," and on to the next neo-thing;
would Shakespeare have but lived till now
he would have put essence above the means,

but history is often presently amiss:
King Henry VIII with six mates—
if only two, their innocence known,
with but a ticket could have flown.

NOETIC

Everything believed,
not perceived through perceptions
is a mystery,

but through hominal
grasp and comprehension
knowledge is conveyed;

ideologies, patterns of belief
and recorded thought
characterize procreation,

giving way to billions of us,
each with a creed
to live by or discredit.

We're all placed in a spot
on a globe in a group
of others like us, and

are happiest when at last
peace and purpose
together press

the fabric of thought
into feelings that desire attests
is just what we wanted.

NOW AND THEN

All is small in druthers to obsess:

    what is it,
    the revelry
    that one needs

    that makes a freak
    fiend for minutes
    flying high?

    It has a look,
    a face,
    it seems

    you see it
    every day,
    it does not change.

What shape does appetition lend

    to insolence
    with pretty eyes
    without makeup,

    and then when flesh
    is forfeit spent,
    and wrinkles are

    cosmetic laud,
    all is small again,
    insignificant

and life goes on
as a conceded
sum of incidents.

Though we are all uniquely fated

on earth now,
each relative
to our existence,

eternity abates
where we will soon
enough be then—

Azrael,
Apollyon,
they

are waiting:
one is smiling,
one is gnashing!

ONCE

it was an attraction, an active
imagination with no relief
but to wonder if silky brown

would rub off of tan skin
in terrycloth shorts
onto fingers grasping them;

then commitment to
what you know not of,
partaking in new things,

sharing feelings
in the need of nights
full of youth

with another soul
until empathy
became you.

Realizing time skies
you streaked through it
as life intervened,

and throughout its course
once can be cold,
it always goes,

relinquishing necessities
whose reckonings still haunt
the part of you they are—

"How much more is the sorrow
of a second love undone
than the purpose of the first one,

and since having consummated both,
which one is yours now?" Once asks,
but it is the third at this moment.

ONE OR THE OTHER

Mediocrity's always stagnant,
half-kissed, destinies declivity
will only advertise if
savants are not seen as eminent;

talent is perhaps its curse,
to live life superior searching,
superlative so few do fit that
comparison does lack intent.

Fealty more so depends
to whom or on what
your soul commits, and
what you believe to be the truth;

its essence is illusiveness
except when manifest
an act suggests that loyalty
loves selflessness, yet

in the end the best,
the in-between, and
the worst of human beings
will converge for a great

and grand welcoming—
who won't admit
they will find forever—
if not in heaven, then the other?

ORNAMENTS IN TIME

Another holiday arrives,
ornaments in time
are ever present:

decorations of recollections
of loved ones alive
still make one smile;

their respite is a restful place
that dawns like daybreak
on nature's face;

hearts overflowing with love,
and memories of little ones
when they were young.

From whence we came never changes,
or the region, the place,
or the sand in the streets

near the ruddy red river
that just kept rolling
as we left and grew older

to become what we have done
through decades of deeds—
now wiser we see

though we are known as we are today,
our lives are enshrined
as ornaments in time.

PARADOXES

Loyalty like love
owes nothing to exist,
first being bestowed,

but for its vitality
all on earth know,
as day is half

the other night,
to persist insists sacrifice
of self for a better cause.

So oft we are to admit
that having learned
to comprehend

does not always show,
and what we do is different
from what we know:

we confess we love
with reverence,
then cannot seem to honor it—

yet I have scarce
a mongrel to know
that did not love

little as much,
devoted to the good
or bad we are as humans.

POEM

Without a poem, I do not have a friend,
and I need this one today to laugh with:

I did not bloom young, lest I would have died
early thereof, and not loved other's kids;

my legs have never crossed naturally,
and will not without blue jeans on my knees;

I subsist in that which I am writing,
and I'm not bound in the time I'm living;

I've created enough to know that thoughts
are life, and fathered many, wrong and right.

Give me just a little time to convene
with your mind, and it will never be known:

instantaneously, I will conceive
and write this poem of ours if you will greet

it like a cool spring day to spend time in,
recompensed and rested—now with just two

more verses left to live in it, the sun
starts to set, and we say goodbye to time

well spent—but unlike so many other
friends, now gone, you will always have this poem.

PRETTY THINGS

that we can't keep,
we want all the more
and forgo reality

that cannot meet our needs,
as we become an artifice
in a facade of fantasy;

having lost sight,
and numbed by extremes,
we love selfishly,

and must feel to perceive
and touch to think,
veiled in vehemence:

>   daily craving,
>   destitute waiting
>   for the next tryst;

>   ecstasy schemed
>   in a fling
>   into a frenzy,

>   panting in,
>   breathing out,
>   not able to shut

>   your eyes from
>   curving round
>   then popping—

wrung from that crazy love,
there's always something
that you can't have

but desperately need—
true, those of you
without such intents

are better off—to will relent,
and control what you feel
as a passionate euphemist

who will never miss
with more than a thought
what you've never known!

SEPARATE

To feel our without
is worse than if we never met,
for we could never crave
what we haven't experienced;

our exquisite earthliness
we will forever miss,
our lips, dry and separate,
now emotionless, are pale,

and a candle lights
the space in nights
that heretofore we oft ignored,
minimizing it by brushing skin

when the mood was full,
and softness like a blanket
you wrapped me in
till time tossed and

took the hours away,
and all of this is more
than I can die to forgo—
my punishment is to live,

remembering that we said
there would be no end,
and separate now
we yearn for it.

SOME YOU LET GO

I did not spend quality time
while mending there
in your green eyes,

I didn't realize our good
times together
each had numbers—

> what is no more
> the memories still hold,
> some you let go.

We were then friends, every weekend,
seeking what we
could get for free;

the moments and the revelries
spent in instants
long since have ceased—

> what is no more
> the memories still hold,
> some you let go.

They called you Ode and Pappy Zipp,
but to me you
were mythical,

fought in the war and played guitar,
and I sought to
be like you were—

what is no more
the memories still hold,
some you let go.

So often we are remiss, and
with deft defense
still hollow hold

wonderful things and one's we've loved
past their deathlike
end with a mope—

what is no more
the memories still hold,
some you let go.

TALL IN MY YESTERDAYS

(To TB)

Your picture is now another
face on a website page—

    in time before
    in a '68 Chevy
    you taught me why

    you were a girl
    and I was a guy
    in less than five minutes;

    experiencing new
    things I was afraid
    to commit to

    that led me
    like a lapdog
    after a treat.

Now despondent through
decades of deeds I lack intent,

    wandering,
    each remiss
    is a trail in time;

    I have no age,
    I cannot find
    my way

to or from,
it does not matter,
I have become

what was,
so much loved
the past defends—

gone thereafter, the red of the river,
I was tall in my yesterdays.

THE ABSOLUTE IDEA OF IT

I thought myself a savant loyalist
to absolute truths and good intents,
but erred again with what I had missed:

I wanted her as mine, with best intent,
and in a chapel we said we did
until I was not Arthur, and her, not Guinevere;

I voted to elect, to put someone in charge,
and then watched others bicker
for months that the outcome was wrong;

I sought to get a vaccine, but hesitated
because technically they are proven
scientifically, but not vetted.

With common sense we comprehend that
there's always more than acknowledgement,
and what we believe becomes evident,

but in the end reality depends, so
we each have our own, and just can't condone
the absolute idea of it!

THE HOLLOW

Where would I be
without the hollow,
the hole through me

is not round
and contours
shapes and things

that never change:
the arch of mornings,
the musk of love

now in dreams
that recreate ways
of without differently

than full serene,
and to hollow men
little smiles never seem

to matter before
they are lost—
then what is void

can only searching
be filled new
to full felicity,

only make it so
before age owns
life in instants,

nearly through,
passing assisted
in memories

that we hope
we do not need
because they are gone.

THE LOT OF LIFE'S WAYS

begins with where we have been placed,
and with what name and genetics
from which race we have been given,

ancestors to act and look like
and descend from—suddenly we
start to become unique, and at

first it's all about us fighting
with our siblings to acquire things
that we want and that we can keep

while growing into who we'll be—
so strange is life that while were young
we aren't able to perceive the

reasons why we are alive and
make selfish mistakes we'll always
regret tending their angst, feeling

dire as time again leaves past cares
to desperately dwell upon them
as it lapses into how we

have spent it, looking past smiles and
feeling sad when love lies latent
and we welcome it with vignettes

of how passion feels indigent
as the use of the world loses
its way, and like a family

dead and gone, the last remembers
good things about the lost the most
so they can be happy like then,

until at last what has passed pales
to what will be when we believe
there is a plan that does not wrest

our souls with death, and we can be
lovely without decay's intent
and fade into freedom's far rest.

THE PAST WE LOVE THE MOST

Cobblestones, the red
of bricks in streets
you've seen before
you see now remembering

in instances, traveling space
in mental ways to small places,
you are there, you think
like then, viscerally,

in a state of innocence
regrets and discontents
and their feelings spring upon you,
conveying what they mean

in little bits, while opportunities
have now become realities,
and blessings sent in multitudes
have now accrued through the years.

The days of life to each are lent
in measured lots that are quickly lived,
but treasured only after being spent,

and though we look to future fortune
and happiness now that we are old—
it is the past we love the most.

THE SAME

What is normality, but
the perceptual equivalence
of external existence
after observing it,

the at-this-moment niche
of activities spent—
often the same, but
sometimes with variants,

like how a person acts
can mask who they are,
and malevolence conveyed
is oppositely obtained—

what then is normal
if both are part
of different aspects
of the same thing?

What is natural
cannot be contrived,
and amidst culture and race
we are presently placed

while striving to survive,
each of us will achieve,
in some way,
something unique,

and live as hominal
ephemeral beings
tilting toward eternity
and the expiry of earth—

while despite in some ways
we are different,
we are the same, and
in His image meticulously made.

THE WAYFARER

I seek out the truth in time-bound
vicissitudes prescribed in nines;
the compendium of life
multiplies until a measured mass
of platitudes prescribe change,
the type you never notice
in the mirror until someone
says that you are not the same.

My mind is a hive of better times,
better days, before maladies became
a second self with separate friends
that congregate in packs on weekends.

Always traveling, I reach for the eternal,
the little bits of it in temporal things:
coral coastlines and caped shores,
their sandy floors serve as borders
between now, the ancient has been,
and the vatical secrets of venues
that history has long since claimed;

through groves and meadows green,
like a hominal breeze I flow through days
and end in evenings, quite serene,
the thrushes and the waxwings wait
and nestle in the live oaks, late
in the twilight before dark, before
the stars consort with the night—

but the night is holding on to me
and I am still traveling
inexorably to the great divide,
the reckoning of nature, time,
and human beings with all eternity,
and I don't know when I will arrive
but my pace is quickening, and I
am ready for the end of earth
and a celestial welcoming.

THE WISP OF INNOCENCE

I began as we all do,
before I knew
that youth was vestal
and life was large.

I was stalled from ripening
by baseball, bulldogs,
and model things—
what could I do in a real car?

I began to feel different
in minutes, little bits
of slender wants,

peeping for a quick fix,
excited,
but not ready for it.

The tales of fervor
from older boys
that blue-jean shorts

and halter tops
quickly come off
did but agitate curiosity,

and I was naturally
this way more pure
than I have ever been,

only now to look back
on what I had yet to waste—
the wisp of innocence.

THE WRIT

I left when I was young and beauteous
so that I'm remembered as such,
and lived in the moments to become eternal,
then lived in the past until I became ghastly
and old to anyone who looked at me.

I've done stupid things,
but had no excuses without the drink,
and tried to amend wrongs with fiends
to whom apologies mean nothing,
and spent weeks worrying.

I've let life happen as a welcoming,
and became half of what I was not
ever intended to be,
only to realize that my body
houses just an interim of me.

I've asked my maker for favors,
for the world did not evolve from
primordial chaos, and surmised that life
is a sacrament, for if it is not, then
I have defiled myself by living it.

I've been defined by the perceptions
of the reflections of others' beliefs,
and became emotionally
associated with their extremes
and what I loved about them for me.

I was told I should not before I did,
and then became sufficiently fearless
to become dumb and foolish
enough to love sin—then again,
we're all freaks for what we need.

I've fantasized about what I could not have,
never realizing what I could get,
and I've been wrong but never in doubt
that more of yourself
means less of others for you to consider.

I've tried to forget what I took
for granted after it went missing,
and used up kindness but never returned it
making other's move on
only to love what was left.

II

I have not yet arrived, but have become
who I should have been, yet still search
for the meaning of life, and for why
I've been given better opportunities
than most who have spent time on earth—
only to not take advantage of them.

I've loved unintentionally
two or three others
through subconscious abstractions
and psychotic dalliances
with reverence and counterfeit
constructs of my true love.

I've partook of nights that never dawned,
and tried to replace what I can't forget
with facsimiles of semblances,
while the music of my time
was poured out and drank down
by 1979.

I've been smart enough to assimilate knowledge,
and wise enough to understand why,
remembering that thoughts and wants
are precursors to actions,
and if down to either-or, blood
always has priority over someone else's love.

I've held on to sand
tightly in my hands, and
watched time slip through them
while searching to discover
that light and shadows exist in our lives,
but only one can be hallowed.

I write autonomously using language
and symbology to expound
upon realities, to be convincing,
but artifice is far more appealing,
and decadence more prolific
than righteousness and decency.

I've lived long enough to see
the beautiful things of my century
become ornaments of the past
and future reveries,
and it's not always true
that you'll die as you've lived,

for my grave I have dug
and I have died a thousand times,
never to have slept in it—then
when I finally forgo earthly form
I will have transformed,
awaiting new anatomy and raiment.

VENERATION

Where are you but in my bosom
with blue-green or pretty brown eyes:
a vesper to attend worshiping,
my recompense never indemnified;

innocence and wonder mixed,
starlight is the death of dark;
slim to medium, I could not confer
a shape to what I chose not to impart;

gerrymandering, each thought competes,
the you that is me with the you that is not
ever to be adored or honored—
at least I know who your mother wasn't.

WE CALLED IT LOVE

It arrived quite young—I jumped
but knew not how high
until I came down,

crashing in the absence of
beautiful brown eyes
radiating bliss,

wondering what exactly
to do as feelings
inundated me;

before I was stricken blind
and could not speak I
felt, I think, that I

was half-a-part of something
God was then doing,
a piece in a plan

made for two stars orbiting,
we were together
for fifty-two weeks,

we were something different,
something wonderful—
we were exquisite;

though we did not understand
we could clearly see
that we could not live

without this wonderful thing
that had become us,
and we called it love.

WE GO AWAY

Where there is no hope,
there is only death
to cradle the bare
and teared muzzy flesh.

The winter is the world,
and all its wars
wrought by man will rage
until their pyrrhic ends.

Where there is no hope,
walks there men,
and broken-baled children
who smile only at night:

    that night
    where they are stars
    and wish upon

    their far-
    reaching scant life,
    and go away—

    hither has
    the human race
    fallen and

    wonders why
    there is still no
    sure answer

to the question,
"Is there mercy
in the grave?"

Where there is no hope,
people believe that life
will end entombed
and because of it spoil.

There is no forever on earth
for as soon as we arrive
we start to transpire, and
our death is only a precursor—

we go away,
but not into the earth,
Adam, then Christ's saving grace
with but belief we earn!

WHEN

your time is gone
what is it,
out of all that you were,
by which you will be known?

Where there is no sea
the night has flown,
and the earth is former
remembrance past

that you will not miss
the remnants of,
for kindred ones
and others loved will be there.

For this journeyman,
all that was worth
has been stitched between lines
in verse

with words that saunter
in their timbre, while
others stall in retrospect
or in reveries rush—

let no elegy parade
or palaver pervert
the purest of a person's worst—
wonder is then permanent.

WHO EXISTS

What is this we have been given:
different places, cultures, races
placed on a planet spinning round
in space while orbiting a yellow ball
so hot only things placed ninety-three
million miles away can survive—
life is sacrosanct: humans, animals,
and nature in ways we still cannot
completely comprehend, and except
for biological, scientific,
and mathematical disciplines
we would still be ignorant
of exactly what life is, and while
the narratives of mankind
have been told through the centuries
of recorded existence, each with
their wonder and woefulness
occurring uniquely, all humans
progressively evolved as if planned
perfectly in providence.

Now the wrath of our ending stirs,
and there are terrible wars everywhere
as fear flourishes and callousness
for life exists as malice abounds
amongst every race for others
who are not the same and live differently
according to their ways and beliefs,
and divisiveness and intolerance exist
in all democracies between liberal
and conservative parties, to the point
that right and wrong is not important
and subject to the ruling parties agenda
and ideologies that are manifest

in every action they commit
to propagate their existence—
a sovereign government cannot persist,
that will be believed to be just,
in societies that so oppositely exist.

So you see, it is what people believe
that is most important,
for this will govern what they do
and how they live their lives—
there are few absolutes on earth,
and we can but yearn
for the peace, amity, and love
that is yet to come for those who trust
in Who put us here,
and the scars that represent the wounds
of what we have done to the earth
and others who have things that we want
remind us of our fall—what we've
wrought is evident, and so is this:

    all entities on earth
    evolve naturally,
    but originally
    did not create themselves
    so wonderfully with
    bodies to exist and
    minds to perceive out of
    primordial ether
    with no design or plan
    or purpose like the roll
    of dice in a crap-shoot
    to win to see what turns
    out to exist—then Who
    could have ordained, devised,
    tailored, and performed this

    Who exists!

WITHOUT

I did not know
that I would become,
and am without knowledge
that I ever was

before I appeared here,
the smallest of wonders
without a name
and in need of a mother.

Only if missing
can without be measured,
so often without pain
it is never considered;

can we ever replace it
or fill the vacuous void
of noble absent needs
so significant to us—

love is superlative enough
that we marvel married in it,
but are never able to sacrifice
completely for its perfectness?

Years ago we were complacent,
now without exists in discontent,
and time will till all of us
it's just a matter of how it's spent—

we are here but for a wisp,
and where less is more
there are no indigent
without in perpetuity.

YOUNGER

I was younger
before I lost,
it matters
to me now

that what the weaker
man of myself could
nihilist boast then,
now can be laid down,

but then the moments
all were shaped:
tall thin seconds
in a round peep;

minutes orbiting
about in a back seat,
and every love
was just another.

Then we lied
to hide our intents,
cheating all
but the urchin years,

past the Methodist church,
past innocence—
the merry times
were all there was,

and where no nefarious
thought still yearns
I hunger,
why the wrongs,

but knew their fill
that I then younger
am thankful now
their lessons to have learned.

REFLECTIONS IN THE MIRROR

(Consider these attentively, for poorly is an incensed life their offering.)

On Division:

Subjugation's elixir is unity, and its cure is *agape* love.

Cultural oppression suffers to exist in united opposition.

If discontent, a dissident will soon exist, and an outcast always turns to things that won't last.

Attentive listening to differences thereof reveals collective truths.

Leisure and luxury are not afforded equally.

The ravages of war will always abhor, and people are pawns to the artifices of it.

Don't fight at the behest of someone else.

How can one feel at ease, and rest in peace, when the world around them is crumbling?

Any loss of an innocent life because of an act of violence is an atrocity.

On Creativity:

Creativity and craziness are comrades.

Talent can supersede addictions, but not for long.

Creativity must have freedom to flourish.

All great writers in their prime had yet to find the amity they were seeking.

Art should not preselect its audience, but without one was created in vain.

Ideas subsist on their own, and are waiting to arrive.

Thought is but one power passing into many forms, and is independent of any effects it creates.

On Life's Lessons:

Common sense only exists to those who have it.

Magic is an illusion of a miracle.

If the world is repugnant to you, change it, or go somewhere else.

Psychology allows one to individualize the universe.

Be careful how you state facts, lest someone label you an "ist"!

Numbers never lie, they just don't tell all of the truth.

A picture is not necessarily worth a thousand words; this will depend on whether one is blind or deaf.

There is no personal difference between what one consummates with in their mind, or in real life.

Beware of anything that exists only in your mind.

Money cannot secure you love, but it can make up for it.

You can never truly be sure about someone's personal commitment, until it involves their money.

Much learning taxes one emotionally.

Nothing less than the best, but nothing more than you can afford.

Genius is a rare gift given, while eccentricities can be acquired and expose you to predilection.

If you can read people, don't judge them with your gift.

A half-truth is no better than a half-lie.

True words of the tongue are deceptive to liars, for they know not whence they're from.

Honest people are the easiest to lie to.

Whoever is not willing to seek out the truth may not acknowledge it either.

The truth is not meant for those it will destroy, lest life be taken away by honesty.

Precious little that is beautiful is spared from humanity.

If you're going to reek of mediocrity, do so arrogantly.

If you can't find your drink, you don't need it.

Dogs don't live as long, lest they feign themselves like humans.

Anybody who loves dogs can't be that bad.

It's always the people who you dislike that help you learn the most about yourself.

Never use someone else to appease your mistakes.

Always honor innocence.

Never try to logically empathize with an emotional issue.

The difference between correction and criticism is in the application.

The correct answer to the question, "Is the glass half empty, or half full?" is "Both."

Facts are rarely objective since they have to be subjectively interpreted; therefore, one is entitled to not only their own opinions, but their own facts.

Subjectivity is a father with an objective child.

Vanity is never cheap.

Character is easier kept than restored.

A promise is only as good as the character of the person who makes it.

A wicked woman who is beautiful is not, and a mad man loves only himself.

Behind every good man is not necessarily a good woman, but there may be one that lies.

Men who do not wield the lure of their eyes will succumb to them blind.

A major part of man is his understanding, or lack of, of women.

If you are not loved for who you truly are, you will become someone you are not.

To love is not enough if you cannot revere and honor it.

If love is not the intent of your partner, then death will be a truth you discover.

Love does not require like.

Love, after it is established, becomes a choice.

Be careful what you call natural.

Our destiny chooses us, unless one decides to humanize it.

You deserve what you tolerate, and when good people do nothing, evil prevails.

To regress is to admit that you have not learned.

As we get older, mistakes made have greater consequences.

Who is ever truly free, except those devoid of possessions, passions, and fears?

Fools die many times, and one should overlook their insults.

Negligence and arrogance are old friends.

My regrets consist in the facts that there were only a few aspects of life I could attend to.

Variety may be the spice of life, but *agape* love is its intended essence.

Agape love is only completed when it is shared.

If I confide in you, only let the faithful know.

The journeys are the rewards of life, but often lead to misadventure.

Endeavor not to waste occasions in haste.

Find a greater purpose.

You can repeat the past, but it will never be the same.

There is no greater solace for a wayfarer than in the bosom of nature.

Travel humanizes a distant man.

I never visit graves—there will be time enough when I'm in one to greet others.

People ignore things that ignore people.

Civilizations go away, and each epoch of time is uniquely arrayed.

On Leadership and Authority:

A balance of command and compassion makes for a better leader.

Intuition is king in a rational kingdom.

The desire to understand is more important than the desire to lead.

To conquer is easier than to govern.

A hero's calm, or a coward's resolve, can save the day.

Never dishonor what you cannot do without.

With respect comes revile.

Just because a majority of people agree on what to do does not make it the right thing to do.

It is not just your choice if another's life depends on it.

Essence is superior to eminence, as fealty is superior to fame.

Do not judge others because of their destiny, and kings to are made of flesh.

Government servants for the people become slaves to the system as politicians.

More government means less freedom, and more people means more chaos.

A committee of nations will never be truly united.

The fairest constitutions and the finest laws are frameworks at best—still people follow their personal agendas and heart's intents.

Public debt is always at the expense of its private citizens.

Public opinion does not value logic.

Among the masses there is no absolute consensus of anything, and individuality is not a priority.

Compromise to stay alive—dictate to exacerbate.

People cannot be regulated to the point of making them intelligent, and entitlements breed rebellion.

Only a good person can be a good citizen, and a state is only as reputable as its citizens.

Personal accountability is the price for freedom, and liberties must have their limits.

On Human Predicaments:

to not value relationships, but miss them after they are gone;

to sincerely enjoy what you are destroying;

to deify what you want above those you love;

to not have the wherewithal to give your all;

to suffer regrets from your own intents;

to have inner beauty that others do not see;

to marry well, but unwisely;

to write much better than you actually are;

to create for the few when it is the many that
need enlightenment.

I don't know you, but I love you.

I don't love you like that.

I can't love you and still be me.

I need somebody who doesn't need me.

I've loved many, once.

I missed you then.

Just leave, don't say goodbye.

You should leave, yesterday.

I'm happy in my sin.

Innocence left with wings.

I'd rather be shameless than spineless.

I wanted more, but I settled to just be a
spouse.

I've been wrong before, but never in doubt.

I went away, before I came around.

I did, but I never wanted to.

If no one knew you, will it matter how you are remembered?

Some important things to you will never come true.

I told him to go straight to hell, but he took care of that himself.

There is no direction without correction.

It's time for me to change again.

I'm just a good person cursed, and I can't do wrong for long.

So many things I daft considered, I cannot unremember.

It was not lawful, but it was the right thing to do.

I threw away what was right for what was wrong.

On Matters of the Heart:

I never fell in love, it either was or it wasn't.

You are my person.

Such beauty you have brought to me—we must wed again.

As we get old, things go away—I hope that you are the last to leave.

The prospect of death makes the heart grow fonder.

The heart does not see well, and knows not of age.

A friend of the heart will never part.

Crying eyes are the easiest to see.

In the dimly lit night, I should have looked twice.

What is right tonight, may not be so tomorrow.

Is not the love you lost the one you desire the most?

To forget is worse than to have lost, though to remember is not enough.

When a rose does not matter anymore, then love does not either.

Foul mouth, foul heart.

No passion, no fashion.

Passion with only the eyes is lust.

When your passion becomes work, you lose it.

Such is grief, that it cannot be postponed.

We are not responsible for our heart's desires, only the actions taken because of them.

If often of the world to taste, your life will be tears for the years to waste.

Why you are sorry is more important than the fact that you are.

It is possible to be in love with two others at the same time, but you can only be true to one of them.

On Spiritual Discernments:

Your demons are still there, but you should choose to rebuke them.

There is no such thing as a demon, until you meet one.

What the devil fears most is your greatest weakness.

Satan will either pervert, or divert, passion.

Doing a good deed for someone who is evil presents an advantage.

Expectation of others is a pathway to disappointment.

What balance is there without a battle, and mercies are the last to leave it?

Pure madness cannot be cured, only banished.

There is no good way to kill yourself.

Our birthright is spiritual maturity.

Body and spirit can be separated, but spirit and soul can only be distinguished.

People loose site of their inner spirituality, without some kind of outer representation of it.

Secular, we savor our sins, but always God preens His image-ship.

Help Thou me to not be blind to what I cannot see.

I don't know, but I know Who does.

Do not assume a righteous position, but one of discernment.

Premonitions are for the superstitious, and for those seeking the future.

In the presence of the Lord, no evil can take hold.

Praise completes what prayer begins, and you become like that which you worship.

To live is to sleep in time, while to die is to awake in eternity.

The end of time heals all wounds.

More of yourself means less of God.

Sovereign on earth as imaged entities, we ought admit God's eminency!

There is no one true religion, but there is one true God.

The merits of Theosophy mar the virtue of the cross.

With God all are created equal, but that viewpoint has never been held by humanity.

It's not all good, but all is well.

To believe is to have faith, to understand is to wait.

Faith is more important than sacrifice or religious rituals.

Obedience is the highest act of religious faith.

You can have as much of God as you want, but not without personal sacrifices.

Acknowledge the giants of life, but emphasize God.

Many things we lack outside of God are blessings.

God takes away things in our lives that take His place.

Do not confuse God's love with His acceptance.

Be as He would have you to be, a blessing in God's eyes.